BOAT PEOPLE

CARDBOARD HOUSE PRESS
www.cardboardhousepress.org
cardboardhousepress@gmail.com

BOAT PEOPLE
Copyright © 2021 Mayra Santos-Febres
Translation © 2021 Vanessa Pérez-Rosario
Designed by Mutandis

First Edition, 2021
Printed in the United States of America
ISBN: 978-1-945720-19-2
Distributed by Small Press Distribution
www.spdbooks.org

MAYRA SANTOS-FEBRES

BOAT PEOPLE

TRANSLATED BY VANESSA PÉREZ-ROSARIO

1.

boat people

carnes trituradas

tiburón de ónix

pelícano en su salsa

en su volantín de alas y cristal

cactus bebido

muérdago de espina

cuerpos hinchados como moluscos

buscando en el fondo del mar

el cielo

de la boca

que es su vientre.

1.

boat people

mangled bodies

onyx shark

a pelican in their sauce

in their winged and crystal kite

cactus drink

thorny mistletoe

bodies swollen like mollusks

searching in the ocean's deep

for the sky

of the mouth

that's their belly.

2.

ah mi morenita cae

       cae hasta el fondo de los pelos del mar

busca tu sueño   cae

busca tu molusco hambriento a siete manos

ah mi morenita en tiento

y de cristal flaquita

por las acuosas noches sin harina

sin más sal quel salitre

que el vaho de la sal cuando salmuera

cuando sal-moneda que exilia   y

       provoca podrirse a la carne de tan poca

                   cae

caspa de carne   cae

ras en la cresta de las olas

     marea en marea morenita

cae

      cae

         cae

y dale de comer a todo pez.

2.

fall oh my morenita
          fall to the ocean's deep where hatchets are buried
fall   in search of your dream
seek your hungry mollusk by touch
with seven hands   morenita mía
crystalline and slender
for all those watery nights without flour
which is no more salt than saltpeter
the salt's briny breath
when salt-coins lead to exile   and

                              so quickly hasten the body's decay

                                                            fall

scales of flesh   fall
verging on the wave's crest
          tide after tide morenita

fall
                    fall
                                   fall

and feed all fish.

3.

el aire falta

va faltando

y continúa el viaje hacia

la ciudad ilegal al fondo de los mares.

indocumentado el alvéolo

explota en canción de melancolía.

el aire va faltando

pero cuál la diferencia con arriba

si arriba falta todo lo demás

lo demás para el caldero y para el pecho

lo de para los bolsillos y los ojos

fríos y callosos de tanto andar

                  esperando

falta el aire

falta

va faltando.

entre las algas brillan unas lucecitas.

quizás allá al fondo sobre

lo que aquí asfixia.

3.

air is lacking

wanting

so the journey goes on

to the illegal city in the ocean's deep.

undocumented alveoli

explode in melancholy song.

air is wanting

but what's different on the surface

if on the surface everything else is lacking

everything for the cooking pot and for the breast

for the pocket and the eyes

cold and calloused from so much walking

                  and waiting

air is lacking

wanting

still wanting.

a few lights glisten among the algae.

maybe in the ocean's deep there's an excess

of everything that suffocates here.

4.

ah sí mi morenita   véndeme tu carne por un beso

por un papel que diga que naciste

véndeme tus profundidades de molusco

tus cositas saladas, véndemelas

para la grasa de los griles que te esperan

para los mapos que van secando el mar de las casas

como tumbas

(el mármol morenita)

y los pelos recortados y pintados de firefighter red

el arrullo de los helicópteros en medio del mar

véndemelo todo en esa carne

tan tuya

tan sebo de tiburones

tan tigra

tu carne desvelada en el fondo de las costas

de las embarcaciones que te traen hasta el

estacionamiento

donde te compro.

4.

oh yes my morenita   sell me your body for a kiss

for a paper that says you were born

sell me your mollusks deep

your salty little things, sell them to me

for the grease on the grills that await you

for mops drying the sea from the houses

like tombs

(of marble morenita)

hair coiffed and painted firefighter red

helicopters humming at high sea

sell it all to me that body

so yours

so shark suet

so tigra

your body sleepless at the base

of the vessel transporting you seaboard to the

wharf

where I buy you.

5.

indocumentado 4

con un cuadro de prócer en la balsa

se tira al mar.

en la jaba lleva agua

lamparita de pilas

un hambre que va para cien años y

cuerpo que la resiste

en la jaba lleva

una rabia vieja

sin nombre y sin culpables

(tantos son los que se le olvidan)

mareada indumentaria del azul.

un haz de tiburones a la saga

    le muerde ese sueño tan lejano.

     su carne percudida en sal

le asegura que jamás se pondrá viejo.

todo tiempo se detiene

en medio del mar.

indocumentado 4 teme jamás arrugarse

mete la cabeza entre las aguas.

lleva el presentimiento de una costa

y el susto de sus guardianes

¡allá!

los ojos de onda corta

5.

undocumented 4
with a picture of a national hero in the raft
he plunges into the sea.
in a sack he brings water
a battery-powered flashlight
a hunger that stretches a hundred years and
a body that fights it
in the sack he harbors
an old rage
nameless   without culprits
(so many he can't recall)
dressed in dizzying blues.
a pack of sharks in pursuit
                    gnaw at his ever-distant dream.
                        his salt-corroded body
assures him he'll never grow old.
time stands still
at high sea.
undocumented 4 fears he'll never wrinkle
dips his head into the waters.
haunted by the premonition of a shore
and the fright of its guardians
there!
shortwave eyes

transistores de barnículos de cal

los ojos desorbitados pararrayos

creen que ven

una franja verde y firme

donde un pie al fin puede hacerse de su senda.

pero no

es tanto el mar.

indocumentado 4

se seca lentamente el espejismo

y las gotas de sal

que le van aguando los retornos.

transistors of calciferous barnacles

disoriented like lightning rods, the eyes

think they see

a firm green strip

where a foot can finally make its way.

but no

there is so much sea.

undocumented 4

slowly dries himself of the mirage

and the salt drops

dilute his returns.

6.

helicóptero

heliotropo

elemento de hélices yerto

eolio de himeneos

óptimo helio de himen escindido

hemisferios de un ojo insecto

eleóptero de acero

eco etéreo y férreo de óleos coaptados

eso

un eón que elucubra

un egeo sol egregio en otro estanque

céfiro de hélices y espejos

helicóptero

heliotropo

elemento

óptimo espectro de perseos

que ofrendan sus carnes incendiadas

al pie del mar.

6.

helicopter

heliotrope

rigid metal helix

aeolian nuptial song

supreme helios of severed hymen

hemispheres of an insect's eye

steel oilcopter

ethereal metallic echo of co-opted oil paintings

there

an eon contemplates

an illustrious aegean sun over another pond

zephyr of helices and mirages

helicopter

heliotrope

metal

perseus's prime specters

offering their bodies ablaze

at shore.

7.

en el vientre de los nuevos animales

lapachando

entre cajas de carnada

y combustibles transparentes

indocumentado 7

vomita para saberse vivo.

la octava vez dio fauce contra las paredes

dentro del vientre de este animal de madera

casi cae a la gran tripa del mar

y de ahí   carnada

y de ahí   avechucho metálico

con aspas sobrevolando a ras de sal.

de una panza a otra lo tiraron

de una panza a otra

y luego fue desecho en las orillas.

indocumentado 7 vuelve al fondo de las cajas

vomita

por novena vez.

aún da fe de que está vivo.

7.

in the belly of new beasts

wading through mire

between boxes of bait

and transparent combustibles

undocumented 7

vomits to find out he's still alive.

it's the eighth time hitting mouth to walls

in the belly of this wooden beast

almost falling to the sea's great entrails

and from there   bait

and from there   metallic sparrow hawk

with blades hovering over salt brim.

from one belly to another they flung him

from one belly to another

and then discarded him on the shore.

undocumented 7 returns to the bottom of the crate

vomits

for the ninth time.

there's some hope he's still alive.

8.

flota mi morenito
tu cuerpo lleno de cangrejos alimentados
panza arriba flota
como la yola que te tiró en sobrepeso
a la fauce azul
                    alafau sea sul
panza arriba
sonrisa tuerta de andar trinco y mojado
con los ojos picado de granpez.
te falta un dedo   morenito
te falta   tiguere
la palabra que decías cuando entonces
y los planes
la mitad de la camisa
te falta   varón
un canto de tu precioso molusco
al que le crecen respiraderos de coral.
moreno
ay mi morenito
pero tú flota
panza arriba   vuela
por la ciudad de indocumentados
que se retuerce
a la fauce azul y dulce fondo
deste traicionero mar.

8.

float my morenito
your body full of feasting crabs
is buoyant, belly-up
like the yawl that tossed your excess weight
into the blue maw

                      intothe bluem aw
belly-up
crooked smile from walking stiff and wet
with eyes stung by magnificent fish.
you're missing a finger   morenito
missing   tiguere
the words you shared back then
your plans
only half a shirt   varón
you're missing
your precious mollusk song
where breathing coral grow.
moreno
you drift
oh morenito mío
belly-up you   soar
through the undocumented city
thrashing
in the blue maw and sweet deep
of this treacherous sea.

9.

tiburón de ónix

control de acceso

esta otra isla donde prometen una casa

una parcelita al menos

donde comer y dormir.

habrá sitio para llegar después del trabajo

después de haber comprado tantas cosas.

habrá sitio para poner la radio alta

rascarse los zapatos

la vida que es la piel de cambiarse el nombre

y parecerse al tipo del papel.

tiburón de ónix

un carrito que viaja por las calles de esta ciudad

rumor de olas domésticas como un jardín para visitas

dientitos que muerden sólo en sueños y no descuajan carne

la carne libre de soldados

libre de detractores

libre de gente niña

vendiendo su flor de pielcarmín

para poder pasar.

tiburón de ónix

control de acceso

pasen yolas y llantas y balseros

a esta isla de espejismos pulidos

9.

onyx shark

controlled access

to this other island that promises a house

a small plot of land, at least,

where one can eat and sleep.

a place to go after a day's work

after having bought so many things.

a place to turn the radio up loud

to wipe your feet

a life where your skin changes its name

to look like the guy playing the role.

onyx shark

a tiny cart moves through the streets of this city

rumbling of domestic waves like a garden for visitors

baby teeth chew only in dreams and do not tear flesh

the body free of soldiers

free of detractors

free of little people who

sell their flower of carmine flesh

to be able to cross.

onyx shark

controlled access

boats and tires and balseros cross

to this shimmering island mirage

que cumple con su hambre
y promete no morder . . .

pero ñam.

that obeys its hunger

and promises not to bite. . .

but chomps.

10.

la costa allá morena por la noche

luz   luces

ojos de coastguard adormecido

huele a tierra

a un dolor cansado que muerde en el costado

hay que tirarse al mar

braceando   huele a más fango

a alimentos gruesos y mojados

a rumor de tripas escupiendo

      gongolí de dolor

         un grito de ahogada

            se entromete en el pulmón explotado

     alvéolo

        por

          rosadito

            alvéolo

un cuerpo que se hincha   allá es la tierra

   que se rehondea   acusona   ah morena

     coqueta   abusadora

     que no se deja arribar

un cansancio y una mano (falta un dedo)

    bracea

       dolor jipiando asma

y los bronquios bailando su zumbido

10.

the coast at night morena

glimmering   lights

coastguard with somnolent eyes

it smells like earth

like a tired ache eating at your side

we must plunge into the sea

flailing   it smells more of dirt

thick and wet nourishment

 a buzz of bowels spitting

          wriggling in pain

                    a drowning cry

                              intrudes on the lung exploding

          alveoli

               by

                         rosy

                                   alveoli

a bloated body   there's the earth

          reverberating   duplicitously   ah morena

               coquette   heartbreaker

               who never allows herself to be mounted

fatigue and a hand (missing a finger)

          flails

                              asthma suffering hiccups

the windpipes dancing buzzing

casi ya

la tierra con la panza abierta

                casi ya.

huele a su vientre

lapachoso.

almost there

the earth with its belly open

                almost there.

the stench of its entrails

mire.

11.

cambiar de nombre

de células de identidad

cédulas de igualita celda

dos por dos

con cable en las manos

célula de grito y edad

procedencia

rito

y otra vez al mar

a cambiarse el nombre

células que idéntico se generan

helios y sol egregio con aspas

de libélula

rémora y un corral

más fuerte quel papel

      aprisionando

una foto dos por dos que atrapa   mueca

de manos con cable a la espalda

a panza de perrera con pestillo

a punto de partida   otro corral

y de nuevo al mar

crédula de identidad

selva de agua

11.

to change names
cells and identity
IDs to an identical cell
two-by-two
with tied hands
a cell of howling aging
provenance
ritual
and once more to the sea
to change names
cells identically become
helios brilliant sun
with dragonfly dartings
remora and a cage
stronger than the paper frame
          imprisons
a two-by-two photo that holds   a grimace
hands tied at the back
belly-latched like a kennel
on the verge of leaving   another cage
identity unquestioned
and once more to the sea
a watery wilderness

con su ciudad enorme de muertos

hinchados en sal.

with its enormous city of the dead

swollen in salt.

12.

tinta para este poema sobre   dejar una isla

de antiguos tontonmacoutes   cielo mediocre

de nuevos tontonmacoutes

que ni para comer

ni para un solo sol de árbol ni maleza en combite.

no hay perros que ahuyenten el derroche

de avisar la llegada de tu muerte.

negra tinta que

sólo un carrefour hecho de agua esta vez

hecho del ojoloco y salitre y ola

aguante los mil pedazos de tu pecho de cartón

        cuatro llantas

                lo que flote   negresa

lo que vuelva invisible esta locura.

los guardianes del cementerio tienen chalecos contra balas

y tú nada

ni una garza que suba al cielo

para hacer llover sobre la yola.

naufragar

sería un beso de las algas

una camita como el caillo entre tus piernas

que ofreces

cuando no queda ni una lágrima qué beberse.

12.

ink for this poem about   leaving an island

old Tonton Macoutes fools   mediocre sky

new Tonton Macoutes

nothing to eat

not even a single sun tree or mangrove in combite.

no dogs to chase away the excess

heralding your death's arrival.

black ink at

crossroads made only of water this time

of wild-eyes and saltpeter and waves

bearing the thousand pieces of your cardboard breast

        four tires

                        whatever floats   negress

whatever makes this madness invisible.

the cemetery guardians have bulletproof vests

and you   nothing

not even a heron rises to the sky to

make it rain on the yawl.

shipwrecked

it would be a seaweed kiss

a little bed like the moss between your thighs

your offering

when there is not even a tear left to drink.

no existe

ni tinta hay

para describir

tu viaje.

there's nothing
not even ink
to describe
your journey.

13.

queda el mar

detrás de su mitad de isla

en el justo medio del arco que dibuja la macana

encontrando sangre tierna en el centro de su carne.

el mar para hacer el humo del sustento

para lamer al menos

la sal de hierro

que queda detrás de una estela

de balas perdidas.

queda el mar

que apunta por los montes   por ciudades

a dos pasos del arrabal.

los ojos

saben que allá lejos   a su otro lado azul

existe gente que come

GENTE QUE COME

que duerme bien a sus orillas

y hasta sueña.

¿cómo hacer

para llegar al mar?

para no rendirse justo a la mitad

de esa trayectoria que traza el sueño

        que es comer.

13.

the sea remains

behind his half island

smack in the middle of the macana-etched arc

he finds fresh blood deep in his flesh.

the sea makes smoke of all sustenance

to lick at least

iron salt residue

in the wake

of stray bullets.

the sea remains

points to mountains   to cities

creeping into suburbs.

eyes know far away

on the other side   of this blue

there are people who eat

PEOPLE WHO EAT

who sleep well at its shores

and even dream.

how to

reach the sea?

and not surrender midway

on the voyage hunting the dream

        to eat.

14.

negra flor de agua   morenita

cuál el remitente de tu calle

cuál la dirección de tus mareas

de ti sale el cielo que es un llanto.

tú eres mi naufragio   yola mía

tú eres mi viaje

allá al fondo verde el alvéolo

carga cuanta alga

dejas anidar en tus costillas.

allá al fondo desta lengua

los dedos de tu sal

          morena

son siempreflor de costa tan ajena

tallo de documento inmarcesible.

el trajín de tu carne

rompe en sombra

contra las olas que mecen cada pétalo en tu piel

el trajín de tu carne   abandonada

busca su remitente y yo no sé

          a dónde enviarla

a qué calle   morenita

a qué cuadra de qué barrio de cristal

donde esperen el aviso de tu muerte.

ay   morena

14.

morenita   black water flower

what's your return address

what's the direction of your current's flow

out of you comes the sky that's a cry.

you're my shipwreck   my yawl

you're my crossing

there in the green deep the alveolus

lays as much algae

as you'll allow a nestling in your ribs.

in the deepest recesses of this tongue

the salty sweat of your fingers

        morena

are everblossom on so foreign a shore

remnant stem of an unfading passport.

your body's swaying

breaks in the shadows

against the waves that rock your skin's every petal

abandoned   your body billows

in search of its home address and I know not

        where to send it

to what street   morenita

to what block of which neighborhood of glass

where they wait for the news of your death.

oh   morena

morenita mía

negra flor de agua

el naufragio de tu carne y tu suspiro

es el naufragio desta sal.

morenita mía

black water flower

your body's wreckage and your sigh

is this salt's shipwreck.

15.

sin documentos

de nombres ya cambiados

no se llaman como flotan   impostores

no son para dar de comer a las gaviotas

y ahí están

reventados por las costas del islote.

de tripa abierta tan azul

que brilla como peces contra el sol

y no son

ni para comerse los pelícanos

y ni para beberse el agua de los mangles

pero díselos tú

a ellos

en patuá   en tiguere   en congo   o en caribe

rebotando de susto contra yolas pescadoras

enredándose de greñas en las hélices

y flotando por ahí

tan campana

tan nísperos de agua reventándose por dentro.

son así   sin sus labios

una sonrisa de encías donde crece el coral

son un llanto muerto por ahí

espantando al que más

y en la yola

15.

without papers
identities borrowed
floating under forged names   imposters
they're not meant to be food for seagulls
and yet there they are
burst open on the islet's shore.
guts so blue
glistening like fish against the sun
and they're not even meant
to be eaten by pelicans
or swallowed by mangrove water
but you go tell them
tell them
in patois   in tiguere   in congo   or in caribe
ricocheting in fear against fishing yawls
hair tangled in propellers
and floating around
like a bell
like watery naseberries bursting inside.
like this   lipless
a gummy smile where coral grows
a dead cry out there
raising fear in most
and in the yawl

el silencio sueña con ahogados legendarios

que halan

a donde tienen su palenque.

a ver   díselos tú

la sal no se hizo para ésto

un cuerpo sobre la arena

no debe estar así   tan desprovisto de su piel

a ver   díselos

a ellos

en patuá   en tiguere   en congo   o en caribe

el hambre no es para costar tanto.

silence dreams of the legendary drowned

who lure

them to their palenque.

so   tell them

salt was not made for this

a body on the sand

shouldn't be   so bereft of its skin

so   you tell them

tell them

in patois   in tiguere   in congo   or in caribe

hunger shouldn't cost so much.

16.

¿cómo es la ciudad de tu muerte   mulata?

dime   ¿por dónde pisas

a la hora del barlovento de   metal?

¿cómo barres las olas de la calle

para que no te vengan a dejar frente a tu casa

basura de mar?

las latas que recogerás allí en tu muerte

y las que venderás por libra pal centavo

¿qué carro coges?

¿qué chevy del 78 y con problemas de ignición?

¿cuántas sopas de alga con pelícanos habrás hecho

pa llevarle a la vecina

y cuántas rumbas   sokas   bachatas y danzones

oirás por la radio en burbujitas

esperando que pase el submarino o el atún

que va hacia el Canal de Panamá?

¿cómo limpias casas de indocumentados que se han

hecho ricos ahuyentando pescadores?

dime   mulata

¿cómo es la ciudad de balsas por donde transitas

con tus ojos desnudos al fin

de tanta costa?

16.

how is the city of your death   mulata?
tell me   where do your feet tread
at the windward hour of   metal?
how do you sweep waves from the street
so they'll not leave sea refuse
at your doorstep?
cans you'll collect there in your death
and the ones you'll sell for a penny by the pound
what car do you take?
which 78 chevy with ignition problems?
how many pelican seaweed soups will you have made
to feed your neighbor
and how many rumbas   sokas   bachatas and danzones
will you hear   bubbles on the radio
while you wait for a submarine or for tuna
bound for the Panama Canal?
how to clean houses of the undocumented who've
grown rich by shooing away fishermen?
tell me   mulata
how is the city of rafts you float through
your eyes stripped at last
of innumerable shores?

17.

llegas a la ciudad donde te pierdes

cambiado   más flaco

más lleno de cristal tu ojo

llegas más acostumbrado a la muerte

a los ruidos de motores

al ruido   al infinito ruido de los carros que parecen

                              tripa de mar

llegas más acostumbrado a insultar

con otro recorte

con otros artefactos bajo el brazo

no ves los letreros   no hacen falta

llegas acostumbrado a andar perdido

y sin casa

para seguir trabajando en lo mismo

más a la defensa de un rollito de papeles que mandas

al antiguo hogar

llegas invisible

hace meses que no te miras al espejo

hace meses que caminas sin afeitar

por la ciudad anónima   de brea es tu alimento

llegas y juras que estás en el fondo del mar

no puedes creer lo que respiras

allá lejos

un cachito de esquina con bodega

17.

you arrive in the city where you are lost
changed   thinner
more glassy eyed
you become more accustomed to death
to engine noises
to clamor   to the infinite din of cars like
                                    sea innards
you become more accustomed to insult
with a different hairstyle
and other belongings in tow
you don't see the signs   there's no need
you get used to wandering lost
without a home
to keep working at the same place
more in defense of small wads of green paper sent to
your old home
you arrive invisible
months of not looking in the mirror
months of walking without a shave
in the anonymous city   nourished by tar you
arrive and swear you're in the ocean's deep
you cannot believe what you breathe
far away
a little corner bodega

te recuerda aromas enmendados

llegas

te tocas la verga en una esquina por aquello de

comprobar

que llegaste con ella puesta

que no la olvidaste en el transporte

llegas con otro nombre

con otras residencias envueltas en un papelito verde

buscas la playa por instinto

estás de espalda al mar

hueles una alcantarilla que te recuerda la proa de una yola

y sabes que andas de paso

más raudo que antes

azaroso

llegas y sabes que estás a punto de irte

y que nunca te moverás de lugar.

reminiscent of healing aromas

you arrive

you touch your cock on a corner to

confirm

it made the journey

not left behind in transport

you arrive with another name

and other residences wrapped up in green paper

searching for the shore by instinct

your back to the sea

sewer smells evoke the bow of a yawl

you know you're just passing through

quicker than before

full of dread

you arrive and know you'll soon leave

and never move again.

18.

ah mulato   tu dedo

dónde lo dejaste

enredado en qué hélice   en qué fauce

quién lo conserva de recuerdo en un frasquito de cristal

quién lo usa para carnada con qué pescar tiburones

quién lo apoya en su barbilla para otear pelícanos y

murallas.

acaso   mulato

fue alimento de alguien que se moría de miedo en una

balsa

vadeando algún río

trepando alguna verja

cruzando algún desierto

para cambiar de identidad.

lo tiene acaso algún niñito moribundo que quiso

respirar por tu piel

mientras caía al fondo

                    —mantarraya de sal

las aguas andaban vivas por tu dedo.

las aguas ardían de huella dactilar.

mulato

quién te besó el dedo de cuajo

quién te lo arrancó tierno . . .

los guardacostas te levantaron casi ahogado

18.

oh your finger   mulato
where did you leave it
entangled in which propeller   in whose maw
who preserves it as a keepsake in a small crystal vase
who uses it for shark bait
who keeps it as a chinrest for watching pelicans and
ramparts.
maybe   mulato
it was food for someone dying of fear on a
raft
wading through some river
scaling some fence
crossing some desert
to change their identity.
maybe it lies with a moribund little boy who wanted to
breathe through your skin
as he fell to the deep
                    —manta ray of salt
waters ran alive through your finger.
waters were ablaze with fingerprint.
mulato
who kissed and curdled your finger
who severed it gently . . .
you had almost drowned when the coastguard lifted you

para meterte en el corral
y el documento ausente de tu dedo te traiciona
traspapelado
¿quién te toma huella ahora   mulato
ah?

and placed you in a pen
your finger's missing passport betrays you
mislaid
who takes your print now   mulato
ah?

19.

nueve van tirados en hilera

en la arena con los párpados violetas

nueve van y un día tuvieron

hasta historia de chiquitos

y después fueron nueve

buscando una ciudad donde comprar

todo lo que anuncian los cristales

lo que anuncian las tripas contra el agua.

lejos   los guardacostas

de todas formas los arrestaron

les ataron las manos a la espalda

los extraditaron de su guardarraya azul y amarilla

                    porque

andaban sin papeles flotando por ahí

tirados en la arena.

los retrató un reportero sollozando de susto

tanta carne

al desperdicio del mar.

¿nueve? se preguntó

y también preguntó por sus almuerzos y lloraba

nueve que una vez fueron

nueve sueños de otra costa y de cositas

desas que se compran con dinero.

19.

nine go strewn in a row

on the sand with violet eyelids

nine go and once they even

had a children's story

and then they were nine

in search of a city where they could buy

everything in the window displays

what guts say when they plunge in waters.

far-flung   the coast guard

arrested them anyway

tied their hands at their backs

extradited from their border blue and yellow

                         because

they had no papers and were floating around

strewn on the sand.

photographed by a reporter sobbing in fright

so many bodies

sea litter.

nine? he asked himself

and asked too about their lunch and cried for

nine who once were

nine dreams of a foreign shore and of little things

those little things money can buy.

20.

aquí al fondo danzan concejales

ahogados todos del Caribe

emisarios

de las naciones del pasaje intermedio:

delegados de Costa de Marfil

ciboneyes todavía suicidándose en rituales de mar

disidentes de Trujillo   de Batista   Duvalier

amigos de Mella

prófugos en barcas por Santomás

cimarrones en su yola

traficantes de sustancias controladas

de carnes y carnadas controladas

pescadores peleando contra marinas de guerra

ex-esclavos intentando llegar   a la Guinea de su libertad.

danzan concejales neo-ahogados

de todas estas islas   no es egeo

algo sobrevuela a ras del agua

y los ve

girando lentamente como un vuelo

hasta bajar a las calles

de esta gran ciudad al fondo del mar.

es tiempo de combites allá abajo

lo saben los nuevos nitaínos saltando de las hélices

20.

consuls dance here in the ocean's deep

all drowned Caribbean

emissaries

of middle passage nations:

delegates from the Ivory Coast

ciboneys still committing suicide in sea rituals

dissidents of Trujillo   of Batista   Duvalier

friends of Mella

fugitives in rowboats near St. Thomas

maroons in canoes

traffickers of controlled substances

of bodies and decoys

fishermen fighting war ships

ex-slaves seeking to reach   the Guinea of their freedom.

consuls of all these islands

dance twice-drowned   this is not the aegean sea

hovering above the water something

sees them

spin slowly as if in flight

until they reach the streets

of this great city in the ocean's deep.

the new nitainos who spring from the engines'

propellers grazing the city's border know

de los motores rozando la frontera de la urbe.

lo saben los nuevos panzallenadeparásitos

el hambre llena los ojos de distancia

bala perdida que encierra su susurro en caracola

vuelta sangre contenida

en siete plomos anunciados.

lo sabemos todos

las balas y el hambre son las madres de la sal

verdes ya los concejales

distribuyen sus pasitos arenosos para poder cruzar

la ciudad de banda a banda.

es rito necesario.

llaman a los que vienen a sumarse

y los que vienen a sumarse responden

flotando.

morenitos

      sirenas

reinas de belleza aquejadas de melancolía

sirvientas que dejan a sus hijos en casa de la abuela

negros lisos como anguilas liberados de su rabia

y de vivir arrastrándose con la boca llena de tierra

la mulata con su hijo entre las piernas

ya limpia de tanto dedo

se suma ella también

it's time for combites in the deep.

the new worm-filled bellies know

hunger fills eyes with distance

a stray bullet sigh enclosed in a conch

becomes blood contained

in seven ringing shots.

we all know

bullets and hunger are the mothers of salt

now green the consuls

organize their sandy steps to cross

the city from side to side.

a necessary rite.

they summon those who come to join them

and those who assemble respond

by floating

morenitos

      mermaids

melancholy beauty queens

maids who leave children at grandma's house

black men smooth like eels freed of their rage

of having to grovel with mouths full of dirt

mulata with her son between her legs

now cleansed of the midwife's fingers

joins in too

libre después que cae entre las aguas

no volverá a dudar

saciada quedará su hambre para siempre

y para siempre sus ganas de ver más

que algo finito que la cerca.

es rito necesario.

los concejales saben que el mar es una hembra

que engulle   digo   acoge y siempre ofrenda

espacio para más

que ella es la casa de aquello que no cesa de saciarse

por eso la convocatoria

por eso el puente infinito de cuerpos

que caen

            oscuros caen   ah negresa

            como en estela de detrito evanescente

            que marca la ruta del viaje hacia lo insaciable.

el mar es insaciable

morenito

por eso bailan los viejos concejales.

el baile llama al hambre necesaria

para que nuevos cuerpos emigren

            a esta casa del agua.

el mar es insaciable

free once she falls into the waters

she'll no longer worry

sated forever her hunger

and forever her longing to see more

than the finite things that enclose her.

a necessary ritual.

the consuls know the sea is a woman

who devours   I mean   welcomes and always offers

room for more

she is home to what never ceases to have its fill

it's the reason for the call

for the infinite bridge of bodies

falling

        dark they fall   oh negress

        as a wake of evanescent debris

        marks the journey's route to the insatiable.

insatiable sea

morenito

it's why the old consuls dance.

the dance summons the hunger necessary

for new bodies to emigrate

        to this water's house.

insatiable sea

e insaciables son las estirpes que crecen a su costa

el mar crea cristales que confundimos con fronteras

con cosas que refulgen allá lejos

        y allá lejos nos tiramos   deseantes

seguimos el ritmo de las olas

el son de una voz que susurrante dice

mulata   ay negresa

ven   morenito mío

        ven a bailar que aquí abajo

no hay que apagar luces

ni hablar bajito.

        aquí abajo el hambre no molesta

y el baile no termina

todo es una cosa muy flexible

y muy acogedora

cuestión de dejarse ir

        dejarse ir hasta de plano

verse convertido en una gota

en un sudor de pez que de repente

se lleva una gaviota

y un verdor lejano que recuerda la tierra

a la que nunca pensaste regresar.

esta es tu casa   morenito

insatiable the bloodline stretches along its coasts
the sea creates crystals confused with borders
refulgent things on foreign shores

                far-flung we plunge   yearning
following the rhythm of the waves
the beat of a whispering voice
mulata   oh negress
come   morenito mío
        come dance here in the deep
no need to dim the lights
to speak softly.

        there's no hunger down here
and the dance never ends
all is supple
and inviting
it's a question of letting go
                let go completely
see yourself become a drop
of fish sweat suddenly
swept up by a seagull
a distant green reminiscent of the land
to which you never thought you'd return.

this is your home   morenito

ven   deja que te abrace
al fin estás conmigo
al fin puedo dejarte de embrujar.

come   let me embrace you

at last you are with me

at last I can stop bewitching you.

Migrants and refugees who exist on the edges of U.S. borders are often constructed in the media as figurative threats to the liberal U.S. social body. Puerto Rican poet and novelist Mayra Santos-Febres is known for creating characters in her work who live on the margins of society. In *Boat People* (2005), Santos-Febres chronicles undocumented migration in the Caribbean, challenging the invisibility of migrants, memorializing the disappeared, and offering insights into human making and unmaking. The poems ask us to consider structural inequality and social injustice in the region, while offering counternarratives to sensationalized violence and criminalized representations of undocumented migrants. Whereas much negative attention has been focused on the U.S.–Mexico border, these poems direct our attention to Puerto Rico and the Caribbean Sea as another U.S. border zone. Originally published in Spanish almost twenty years ago, today *Boat People* remains as crucial as ever. Literature has the power to move readers in ways that statistics cannot: in the wake of Black Lives Matter, the migrant crisis at the U.S.–Mexico border, and the ecological and debt crises in Puerto Rico, this collection of poetry is urgently needed.

The title of the book, *Boat People,* is written in English (though the poems are written in Spanish), suggesting that the United States is the destination sought by these migrants. Imagery and words in Caribbean Spanish and Haitian Creole throughout the collection evoke the Atlantic as another U.S. border zone. The title calls to mind not only migrants in the twenty-first century but also those who came from Vietnam by boat in the aftermath of the Vietnam War, and Haitians who risked their lives at sea to escape the Duvalier dictatorship. "Boat people" is a catch-all phrase used to refer to the large number of migrants who leave their homes in balsas, yolas, rafts, and small fishing boats, regardless of whether they are refugees fleeing human rights abuses and persecution or economic migrants in pursuit of a better life. The imagery of "boat people" echoes back to the violence of the Middle Passage and Atlantic chattel slavery. Layered onto this original journey are others, including those made by dissidents of the mid-twentieth-century dictatorships of Duvalier and Trujillo, as well as (in the late-twentieth and twenty-first centuries) those of economic migrants seeking an escape from poverty. Today, emigration has become a survival strategy in the Caribbean.

Puerto Rican literature continues to draw a blank among most American readers and students of literature. Major authors are still unknown, and remain largely untranslated. However, twentieth-century American social values and priorities are visibly imprinted on Puerto Rico's literary history. In 1898, four centuries of Spanish colonialism ended when the United States invaded Puerto Rico. Decades of imposition of the English language, the unilateral decreeing of American citizenship in 1917, economic and social crises during the Great Depression, externally controlled industrialization, unprecedented migration, and ecological contamination are not only part of Puerto Rico's recent history; they are events in America's past as well. The aftermath of Hurricane Maria in 2017 extended this fraught legacy, shedding light on the enduring colonial relationship between the island and the United States.

These poems put on display the anxieties and complexities of the migration crisis, revealing the problems of U.S. occupation, neo-imperialism and globalized power that are mapped onto Puerto Rico and the Caribbean more broadly. Santos-Febres explores the challenges of telling migrants' stories, of documenting the undocumented. Due to the precarious nature of these journeys, the number of migrants who emigrate each year and do not survive to tell their stories is unknown. The invisibility and fragility of these lives is echoed in formal aspects of the poems, which are written mostly in lowercase letters (capital letters and proper names rarely appear), suggesting the travelers' invisibility. Their stories are untold, their names are not preserved. The lack of personal markers also reminds readers that these stories are multiple and varied while also being one in the same. The poems are brief and their short lines highlight the fragile, ephemeral quality of these lives. Set at high sea, the poems dramatize journeys, lives, and dreams that drift to the bottom of the ocean. These verses offer fleeting glimpses of humanity and suffering and pay homage to Black migrant and undocumented lives. A personified sea is the only witness to migrants' journeys, and their stories are often told through the powerful voice of the waters that absorb them.

Apostrophe is used repeatedly as a way to animate the dead. This rhetorical device functions as an intensifier, marking outbursts of concern, attaching forceful emotion to the scenes and events described. The speaking voice in the poems, often the voice of the sea, invokes undocumented migrants in an attempt to turn them into interlocutors, into subjects, either by referring to them in the second person pronoun tú or by addressing them with Black Caribbean terms of endearment (morenita/morenito and mulata/mulato). The voice calling out to these figures often speaks soothingly from the depths of the sea, from a place of love and seduction. Translated into English, these terms would lose the particular quality of care evoked, and the poems' force would be diminished. Santos-Febres uses colloquialisms in Dominican and Caribbean Spanish that resist translation, such as tiguere and varón. To retain the poems' multilingual quality, I have also chosen not to translate Haitian Creole words.

The text's opaque language creates a challenge for translator and reader alike. Faced with the text's impregnability, we are left with its imagery and the sonority of its verses. Santos-Febres confronts readers with a sense of loss, highlighting the inaccessibility of African diasporic memory, invulnerable and irrefutable, yet also out of reach. This dance between meaning that can be grasped and that which is elusive, together with the fragmentary nature of Santos-Febres's imagery, can be described as a cimarrón poetics, which works to create "illegal" and "undocumented" spaces that exist beyond surveillance and policing. A cimarrón poetics resists legibility, instead leaving us with shards of image and sound that give rise to fertile and generative extraterritorial spaces.

The collection contains extensive references to biological elements and human anatomy. Migrants appear on the page reduced to their parts, as abject corporeality. The poems are awash with fragmented bodies and their detached components—flesh, mouths, alveoli, eyes, fingers, feet, bellies, entrails, skin, teeth, lungs, bronchi, cells, ribs, tongues, eyelids—that cannot be contained by their representational space. The reader must seek to make meaning from these disconcertingly dismembered bodies strewn over the sand and scattered at sea. The rhetorical trope by which these relations are configured (and disfigured) is synecdoche, but in these poems, it is impossible to integrate parts into wholes. Loss of bodily coherence is ultimately the loss of coherence as such. The body part, cut off from the totalized body, works to challenge the structure upon which meaning is based. This loss of coherence—this presymbolic chaos—is figured by the body in bits and pieces, which cannot be successfully reassembled as a liberal subject, instead appearing as waste and contaminants against which the American body politic must be protected. Liberal political thought has tended to decipher embodiment in strikingly artificial, antiseptic terms, as always already dignified and integrated. *Boat People* challenges this notion as it manifests the body's suffering, brokenness, and finitude.

The poems in *Boat People* can be read as twenty-first-century elegies. In the modern sense of the term, the elegy is a short poem, usually formal or ceremonious in tone and diction, and occasioned by the death of a person. Elegies frequently move from sorrow to consolation. Historically, the elegy was a meditation on any topic, though it often dealt with themes of love or death. The twentieth-century elegies of Paul Celan's *Todesfuge* are written as a meditation on the victims of the Holocaust. Seamus Heaney's elegies in *Field Work* are written for the victims of political violence in Northern Ireland. Similarly, Santos-

Febres's poems in *Boat People* reflect on the losses occasioned by Caribbean migrations set into motion by wars, environmental catastrophes, and insecurity. Traditionally, the elegy functions to lament, praise, and offer comfort in response to loss. It gives expression to grief and dispossession, exalting its subject by idealizing the deceased and preserving their memory among the living. And elegies console, by meditating on natural continuities or moral and metaphysical values. In *Boat People*, the sea is the enduring natural element: she is primordial, she is siren, she is seductress, protector, and mother, and she is the source of life and death—a terrifying and violent yet nurturing space beyond the reach of the laws and protections of nation-states.

In Caribbean poetry, the sea as a space of radical alterity is a recurring motif. African diasporic memory is deeply embedded in Santos-Febres's sea imagery—the illegal city at the bottom of the ocean, and the blankness and nothingness of open space. In Puerto Rican literature, Blackness is continually displaced and relocated to the water, foregrounding the sea's critical role as witness to the horrors of the Middle Passage. In *Boat People*, Santos-Febres describes new middle passages, the afterlives of slavery. Images of migration by boat carry with them a host of historical narratives of discovery and loss and of successful navigation and return; they capture the redefinition of identities in migration. The Middle Passage has become representative of violence, degradation, dehumanization, and exploitation. The iconic slave-ship image of Africans chained together appears repeatedly in Caribbean literature and iconography. Echoes and reverberations of the Middle Passage are present in *Boat People* in the repeated images of yolas, balsas, and other small vessels transporting Black bodies. The apparatus of slavery—the port, the chain, the scales, and the ship—account for a Middle Passage aesthetic that embeds African diasporic memory in creative expressions that challenge historical amnesia. For Santos-Febres, African diasporic memory and the apparatus of slavery are what produced the modern Caribbean archipelago. This collection, which contains abundant references to the Aegean Sea and Greek mythology, links the Caribbean Sea as a central commercial space that facilitated trade and cultural exchange in the Atlantic, to the site of the origins and foundation of the modern world.

Ship imagery evokes ideas of crossing, movement, migration, and borders. The poems conjure multiple, layered crossings: crossing over from the living to the dead, from one nation to another, from one identity to the next. Santos-Febres creates a "city of the dead"—a space outside time. The city of the dead is eternal like the grave and like the sea that is its home. It is at once a city of ancestors, a place of memory, and a mythical literary place that disrupts European normative views of space-time. It is an illicit, cimarrón space, a maroon space, a space of marronage. There is a tradition of Caribbean poets such as Luis Palés Matos, Julia de Burgos, Aimé Césaire, Kamau Brathwaite, and NourbeSe Philip, who write about the sea as a space of longing, seduction, and creativity. In *Boat People*, written in this tradition, the speaking voice emerges from the bowels of the sea. The sea is a wellspring, she is the source. Entranced travelers plunge, mimicking the suicide rituals of their indigenous and African ancestors who chose death over humiliation and enslavement. The sea nurses and nurtures the migrants. The waters bear witness to migrants' lives, hold their stories, and defend and protect them, providing safe passage to the other side or easing the journey to their final dwelling in the ocean's deep.

ACKNOWLEDGMENTS

I thank Mayra Santos-Febres for trusting me with the translation of this beautiful and moving collection of poetry. I was captivated with the poems when I first read them, and it has been a joy to translate them. The idea for this project was birthed while I was a fellow of the Committee on Globalization and Social Change at The Graduate Center, City University of New York. It was the prompting and encouragement of two members in particular–Joan Scott and Duncan Faherty–which emboldened me to take on this project. I thank my readers and interlocutors: Bobbi Harshav, J. Bret Maney, Kahlila Chaar-Pérez, Roberto Márquez, Wilfredo José Burgos Matos, Régine Michelle Jean-Charles, Marisel Moreno, and Arnaldo Cruz-Malavé. My thinking about this collection is in conversation with other works on waters and oceans such as *Routes and Roots* (2007) by Elizabeth DeLoughrey, *Zong!* (2011) by NourbeSe Philip, *Caribbean Spaces* (2013) by Carole Boyce Davies, *In the Wake* (2016) by Christina Sharpe, and "Toward a Genealogy of Water" (2017) by Rebeca Hey-Colón. I am grateful to Kelly Baker Josephs (editor of *sx salon*) and Rosamond S. King (creative editor), for publishing early versions of the poems "air is lacking," "to change names," and "morenita black water flower." I am grateful to Carmen Giménez Smith, poetry editor at *The Nation,* for publishing a version of "oh your finger mulato." I am especially grateful to Charlotte Whittle, my editor at Cardboard House Press, who believed in this project from the start. My deepest gratitude to David Scott, who listened attentively while I read the poems aloud over and over in search of the perfect word to complete a line.

ABOUT THE TRANSLATOR

Vanessa Pérez-Rosario is a translator and professor of English at Queens College, City University of New York where she teaches U.S. Latinx and Caribbean literatures and cultures. Her translations have appeared in *The Nation* and *sx salon.* She is the author of *Becoming Julia de Burgos: The Making of a Puerto Rican Icon* (University of Illinois Press 2014) which will be published in a Spanish edition, *Julia de Burgos: la creación de un ícono puertorriqueño* (University of Illinois Press 2021). She is editor of *Hispanic Caribbean Literature of Migration: Narratives of Displacement* (Palgrave 2010). She is currently editing a bilingual anthology of Julia de Burgos's collected writings.

ABOUT THE AUTHOR

Mayra Santos-Febres was born in Carolina, Puerto Rico, in 1966. She studied Literature at the University of Puerto Rico and received two postgraduate degrees from Cornell University. She is a professor of Creative Writing at the University of Puerto Rico, Río Piedras and a member of the International and Multicultural Institute of the UPR. She has received, among other awards, the Letras de Oro and the Juan Rulfo, both in the short story genre. She is the recipient of a John S. Simon Guggenheim scholarship (2017) and the Rockefeller Bellagio Center Residency (2018). Her works have been translated into French, English, German, Croatian, Korean, Icelandic and Italian. She is the author of the poetry books *Anamú y manigua* (1990), *The escaped order* (1991), *Boat People* (2005), *Tercer Mundo* (2014-20), and *Huracanada* (2018). She has also published the novels, *Sirena Selena vestida de pena* (2001), *Cualquier miércoles soy tuya* (2002), *Fe en disfraz, Nuestra Señora de la noche, La amante de Gardel,* and the collections of essays, *Tratado de Medicina Natural para Hombres Melancólicos* and *Sobre piel y papel.*

Printed in the USA
CPSIA information can be obtained
at www.ICGtesting.com
CBHW020420021123
1601CB00003B/21